Mountains of Inspiration

Reflections on Climbing Mountains

Carol Deckard

Carol

Printed in the United States of America
by The Old Gypsum Printer, Inc.

First printing, March, 2011

Mountains of Inspiration, Reflections on Climbing Mountains

ISBN 978-0-615-44487-1

Contact author at carold@vail.net or www.mountainsofinspiration.com

Photographs by John Fielder

Editing & Design by John Kempf

Layout by Vincent Hidalgo

Published by Carol Ann Deckard

Acknowledgments

John Fielder, nationally renowned landscape photographer, strikingly captures the wonders of nature through the lens. I am grateful to John for allowing me to display his spectacular photographs in *Mountains of Inspiration, Reflections on Climbing Mountains*.

John Kempf's advice and encouragement helped me to focus and persevere during the development of this book. I am thankful for his support.

Roundup River Ranch will receive a donation of
20% of proceeds from book sales.

Roundup River Ranch's mission is to enrich the lives of children with life-threatening illnesses by providing free, year-round camping experiences with appropriate medical care that are fun, safe and empowering. Roundup River Ranch is a provisional member of the Association of Hole in the Wall Camps and is following a set of guidelines to become a full member that are designed to assure that each member camp provides the highest level of safety, programming and sound financial support. When Paul Newman started the first Hole in the Wall Camp in 1988, he had a simple idea of creating a place where kids suffering from childhood diseases could "kick back, relax, raise a little hell and just be kids." To date, nearly 200,000 children from around the world have attended Hole in the Wall Camps free of charge. Roundup River Ranch will open in the summer of 2011 along the banks of the Colorado River two hours west of Denver and 9 miles north from the Dotsero exit on I-70.

Prologue

The aroma of freshly brewed coffee lured me into the kitchen.
I slipped into my terry robe and knotting the belt around my waist,
wandered toward the coffee maker, poured my morning craving into
a mug and trudged upstairs to my office. Climbing onto a daybed and
snuggling into a nest of pillows, I covered myself with a chenille throw
and drew my knees into my chest. The steaming mug warmed my hands
as I savored each sip, gazing out the window at the sage covered hill.
Rays of light inched their way over the mountain, chasing away the
shadows. A herd of deer rested peacefully in the tall sage that glistened
in the morning sun. My puffy eyes reminded me that I had not just
awakened from a bad dream. The reality stunned me that frosty morning
in December of 2009. I was unemployed.

After celebrating my 53rd birthday and more than 30 years in
the resort business, several of them in Human Resources, I frantically
thought – *What am I going to do next?* I suddenly found myself among
the thousands of other people who were looking for work in a dire
economy. Together we stood at the same crossroad.

Gray clouds rolled in and aspens began to sway while several snowflakes twirled and then melted away on the windowpane. The deer lazily meandered down the mountain and out of sight. My collection of best-selling business and motivational books sat in the middle of the floor packed in boxes. Seeking answers, I selected one, nestled back into the pillows, re-wrapped the throw around me and immersed myself in the pages. Soon, it was dusk. Struggling to keep my eyes open and too exhausted to amble downstairs to the bedroom, I removed my robe and crawled between the sheets, wondering – *How can I reinvent my life?*

Each day, I climbed into my sweatsuit, wool socks, wrapped myself in a chenille throw and voraciously read the books in my library, searching for ways to create my destiny. I took long walks, pondering my achievements and disappointments, rewinding various scenarios in my mind. Eventually, the layers of fear and self-recrimination wrapped tightly around my head and heart began to loosen.

One day, a nature photography book by John Fielder caught my attention. As I slowly turned the pages, the photographs transported me into the wilderness as I recalled my own experiences hiking in the Colorado Rocky Mountains. The images captured the essence of the thoughts and emotions reverberating within, motivating me to write *Mountains of Inspiration, Reflections on Climbing Mountains*.

We come to many forks in the road at different stages in our lives, experiencing disappointments, sorrow and setbacks as well as victories, joy and celebrations. As we confront turning points, mountains emerge on the horizon and beckon us to climb them. Whether we go through moments of rejoicing or lamenting – we have a choice. We can turn back, do nothing or move forward and upward.

Defining moments have the potential to transform our lives – personally, professionally and spiritually. Timeless messages whisper to us. If we listen carefully, we receive the wisdom to learn and grow and the courage to press on. Step into the high country to reflect...

Reflection

Solitude calms the mind like the smooth surface of a tarn nestled below jagged peaks. Suspend time…release tension…awaken your senses and allow thoughts to drift through your consciousness like gossamer clouds floating across the sky.

Only in stillness is our reflection clear. Become aware of a strength welling from within and propelling you forward as "ah ha" moments are revealed.

Wonders are omnipresent – veiled by our busy lives. For the moment, turn off your cell phone and shut down your computer. Resist the urge to respond to the steady stream of emails and text messages. Forget worries, troubles and the pressing items on your to-do list.

In silence, you may encounter a sign – not a dramatic sign like a burning bush accompanied by a deep booming voice emanating from the heavens – but a revelation, warm glow and subtle gravitational pull, enticing you to explore possibilities and discover the miracles around you.

Giant clouds reflect on the glass-like surface of the pond, gliding across the water, blocking the warmth of the sun. Stare at the clouds and more will come your way. Shift your gaze to the patches of blue and in time, clear skies will be ever-present.

Passion

Passion illumines our essence, its flicker glowing from deep within to touch our hearts. To ignore the light is to live in shadows and wonder what could have been. Kindle the flame and dance with your destiny.

Aspens struggle to survive under a dense canopy of pine trees. Their roots require the sun's energy to permeate the earth and stimulate growth.

Step out of the shade. Nourish your soul with light and warmth, and flourish.

Yellow aspen leaves adorn the forest, sparkling like precious jewels in the morning sun.

Brighten the world with your brilliance. Let the gold within you shine!

Aspire

Close your eyes. Envision standing on the crown of a hill, reaching for the moon hovering inches away from your fingertips. Capture and hold that moment. Believe in possibilities. Trust that you can ascend to great heights.

Optimism is a magnetic force that compels us to climb the steep and rocky slopes and achieve our highest aspirations. Use that power to pull yourself up.

Our dreams wax and wane. The moment we conceive them in our imagination, we are motivated. Then doubt seeps into our thoughts and we lose our confidence, procrastinate or stop trying. Have courage and strength to persevere.

Vision

The peaks and valleys of our past glow in brilliant colors. Pause on a crest and observe the panoramic view, weighing what you have learned from your successes and failures. Leave yesterday's burdens behind. Imagine how you want this day to unfold. Allow wisdom to guide you and advance towards the rising sun that shimmers on the horizon, signaling the way to a bright future.

The rising sun enlivens our day with a kaleidoscope of opportunities. Ask yourself – *What can I do today to bring me closer to the summit?* Begin now. Proceed one step at a time.

Visualize your dreams and bring them to life in your imagination…see them in vivid colors…listen to them sing to you in harmony…smell the bouquet… taste their sweetness …and feel the thrill that comes from accomplishment.

Ascend

Be surefooted and move with grace on your journey. Show dignity and respect to those who you meet on the trail.

Leaders are not necessarily those at the head of the herd. Those who influence others assume a responsibility for enriching lives – their family, work environment and community, donating their time and resources for the betterment of humankind. They possess an attitude of abundance, acting with integrity in their personal and professional lives. There is no better time to lead than now.

Our climb may result in exhaustion and stress, triggering poor decisions that can cause an avalanche. Know when to step back, catch your breath and allow another to take charge through the difficult terrain. Be sure that you want to follow the group.

Appreciate

Mountains stand boldly in the distance…a thrilling adventure to conquer…a frightening obstacle to avoid…or a tranquil scene to enjoy from afar. What do you perceive? What does your neighbor see? Value and learn from other points of view.

Alpine flowers paint the meadow. Each blossom illuminates the variegated field with its intricate details and hues.

Praise is a gift. Give it freely. Those who are struggling to grow will bloom with showers of sincere compliments and applause.

Storms

Snow-covered crests vanish into the grey clouds that suddenly appear. A brilliant light flashes across the sky and a loud crack echoes through the highlands. A tree trunk is a target for the static electricity gathering in the air. Charcoal markings remain engraved on the bark from past storms.

Tumultuous events unexpectedly pass through our lives, leaving wounds etched upon our hearts – death of a loved one, illness, failures, harsh words and malicious gossip. The sun will eventually reappear. Light fades our scars.

What if I fail? Harmful thoughts sneak into our consciousness and fog our vision. We lose our sense of direction, blinded by the mist that thickens around us, and become paralyzed – too frightened to take another step, fearing we might stumble and fall.

Breathe deeply…let go of the tension as you exhale. Clarity will come and guide you through the haze.

The road meanders with many twists and turns. We can be deceived by what appears to be an effortless route and tempted to take a short cut. Off the path, flora come to life – tree roots trip us, bushes reach out to scratch us and unexpected dangers lurk around each bend. Remain true to your principles – they are your trusted companion.

Rainbows

After the downpour, bright colors appear arcing across the sky – a vivid reminder of life's gifts. Sometimes it takes a little rain to appreciate them.

Light reflects and refracts on the droplets of moisture in the air. Ponder setbacks. Bend with change.

Show gratitude for the abundance in your life and notice how scarcity begins to diminish. Count your blessings and discover the treasures at the end of the rainbow.

Flow

Our most precious natural resource has the power to carve magnificent canyons by surrendering to the laws of nature. What can you achieve if you stop resisting the calling from your heart?

Continue to nurture your mind, body and spirit. Savor the moments when they are in harmony and you experience inner peace.

Like glacial lakes that melt in the spring and flow into the streams that feed into the rivers that pour into the oceans… generosity is a powerful force. It springs from our depths, cascading throughout humanity.

The human spirit prevails with gifts of love, care and tithing – a cycle that sustains hope and life.

Epilogue

Warm temperatures melted the snow after a long winter of enduring internal storms – the fear and anxiety that accompanies uncertainty. Grabbing my backpack, water and an energy bar, I headed for the wilderness to clear my mind.

The conversation I was having with myself quieted as I clambered over fallen trees and cautiously stepped onto moss-covered rocks that formed a bridge across the stream. The forest came alive – woodpeckers tapping, the chatter of squirrels and chipmunks and the twigs snapping beneath my feet.

My muscles burned as I ascended the steep slope to the top of a ridge. Beyond a meadow of alpine flowers lay a jewel that shimmered in a bowl surrounded by rugged peaks. I strode through the tall grass and climbed onto a boulder resting along the shore. I pulled off my boots and socks and dangled my legs over the edge. The granite radiated heat from the mid-day sun and tension melted as I basked in the tranquility, gazing at my reflection in the still pond.

An eagle soaring above interrupted my meditation. I put on my gear, slid off the rock and continued on the path that led to the mountaintop. The summit drew closer as I slowly trekked across a field of snow. Catching my breath, I stood on the highest point and marveled at the rows of snow-capped mountains that touched the horizon in every direction.

The gray clouds floating above began to rumble. The wind picked up and whipped around me. Freezing rain began to fall, stinging my hands and face. I ran down the hill to timberline and huddled under pine boughs, mesmerized by the crystals bouncing off the earth. Eventually, the hail stopped and the sun reappeared, warming the cold air.

The afternoon shadows warned me to continue down the hill. I began following what appeared to be the trail. Suddenly it disappeared. An eerie feeling came over me when I realized I was alone in the middle of the forest. I looked over my shoulder and up the hill – *Should I turn around?* Obstinacy drove me forward. Afraid of startling a bear, I began to sing. A tree creaked loudly, swaying back and forth. I could only imagine what might be up there clinging to the branches. I sped up my pace and blindly stumbled down the hill.

At last, I found my path and continued on my way, mindfully watching each step. With a renewed spirit, I headed for the trailhead, reflecting on my life and the lessons I have learned.

When hiking, it's critical to stay on the trail to avoid stepping on the delicate ecosystem that is struggling to survive in the wilderness. The footprints we leave behind imprint the memories of the fragile souls we encounter on our journey. Leave impressions that nurture – encouraging words and acts of kindness. Create an environment that will flourish and a legacy that will endure.

About the Author

Carol Deckard lives in Colorado's Vail Valley.
She is currently a consultant in the resort industry,
writing her next book, and continues to climb mountains!

Visit www.mountainsofinspiration.com or contact Carol at carold@vail.net.

Show appreciation to those who have helped you to climb mountains. Lift the spirits of someone who has come to a crossroads in their life. Give them *Mountains of Inspiration!*